THE BUDDHIST CAR

and Other Characters

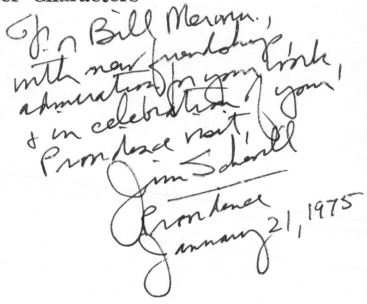

For Bill Merwin,
with new friendship,
admiration for your work,
& in celebration of you!
From here next.

Jim Schevill

From here
January 21, 1975

Books by James Schevill

Poetry

Tensions
The American Fantasies
The Right to Greet
Selected Poems: 1945-1959
Private Dooms and Public Destinations:
    Poems 1945-1962
The Stalingrad Elegies
Violence and Glory: Poems 1962-1968
The Buddhist Car and Other Characters

Drama

High Sinners, Low Angels
The Bloody Tenet
Voices of Mass and Capital A
The Black President and Other Plays
Lovecraft's Follies
Breakout: In Search of New Theatrical Environments

Biography

Sherwood Anderson: His Life and Work
The Roaring Market and The Silent Tomb

Translation

The Cid (a translation of Corneille's *Le Cid*)

THE BUDDHIST CAR

and Other Characters

James Schevill

THE SWALLOW PRESS INC.
CHICAGO

Published by
The Swallow Press Incorporated
1139 South Wabash Avenue
Chicago, Illinois 60605

ISBN (CLOTH) 0-8040-0628-8
ISBN (PAPER) 0-8040-0629-6
LIBRARY OF CONGRESS CATALOG NO. 73-1502

This book is printed on 100% recycled paper.

Acknowledgments are due to the following publications in
which some of these poems previously appeared:

> Antaeus, Saturday Review, The Humanist, Prairie
> Schooner, Counter/Measures, Hearse, Hellcoal An-
> nual One, Pembroke Magazine, Mill Mountain Re-
> view, Western Humanities Review, American Dialog,
> Diana's Bi-Monthly, Release (A pamphlet published
> by Hellcoal Press). "The Glorious Devil at the Dove-
> cot" was written as the Phi Beta Kappa poem at
> Brown University in 1971.

A number of these poems were first published in book
form in Private Dooms and Public Destinations: Poems
1945-1962, The Swallow Press, Inc. "Descartes Composes
a Ballet" was also published in The Dance, The Dancer,
and The Poem, edited by Jack Anderson (Dance Perspec-
tives, 1972).

Contents

To Margot

The Buddhist Car

(A Buddhist, exiled in the United States, dies suddenly
and finds himself reincarnated as a car.)

I

Slowly, I feel myself. Eyes squint at me
Through a long window. Across the glass is lettered
FURY. My skin is growing hard, my bones hammered longer.
My veins flow in glistening wires, tubes.
The curious, glittering people glide in
To touch me. My face is etched with polished lines,
A metal beehive. Singular words sound against
My antique English, *throttle, mileage, accelerator.*
Suddenly, my heart explodes, sparks of energy
Shoot through my bowels. I hum, flow out
To hard streets. I glide on rubber circles.
Children call to me, smile, speak my title.
I know who I am . . . Across my rear puffing fumes
Curve the letters, F-U-R-Y . . .

II

"As the blade of a sword cannot cut itself,
As a finger-tip cannot touch itself,
So a thought cannot see itself . . ."
I cannot see what I think. Male fingers guide
My large-beamed eyes down the road,
A polished shoe presses my sex,
A woman stamps out her cigarette in me,
Children litter my skin with candy wrappers, gum.
A man who liked the touch of silent women,
I echo with female flutes of gossip.
I flee from high, trilled syllables,
Devote myself to winds of motion,
Speed as vision . . . If *nirvana* is kin
To *moksha*, release, that liberating light,
I must learn to feather-float on metal parts.

III

An agony of sudden climbing . . . After learning
Stop and go in warm sun, I spring
Up mountains through ice and snow.
My family's name rolls with gutteral sound:
Mac-Pher-son, a candy manufacturer,
Wearing a cap and red-striped sportshirt,
His brown, jovial balloon of a face
Round over a clouded, blackstemmed pipe.
His wife, Raquel, wears a pleasant mongrel smile
From the melting pot, lined with anxieties,
Her grey hair washed and loaded with spring coils.
They create a friendly team of curiosity,
Poking at facts, investigating objects,
Eager to proclaim the wonder of natural views,
Their two tense, prancing children shaped
Tightly after the parents' investigating passion.
Since I am this family's walls of privacy,
I sense their fear of quicksand loneliness,
Their need to honor, obey the American verb, *to do*.
External action glitters fiercely in their eyes.
To them beauty is a fiery eyeball; it cannot
Sing from ancient unity of body with mind.
A child's voice shrills in my ear, *Sierra, Sierra!*
We search high places. I learn to curve, turn,
Climb on deceptive slopes that ache my parts.
I gasp for distant breath through lung-pumps
That press cooling air against my hot nerves.
Higher! Higher! If such a path wound through
The Himalayas of Wonder, what frenzied light
Could be seen. *Kanchenjunga! Makalu! Everest!*
MacPherson thrusts me into slower motion.
Every sinew strains. I force deep power.
What muscles! My water steams . . . *Sierra! Sierra!*

2

IV

A slight pause on top of the world,
Intense light glittering on my body,
Then a sudden plunging down . . . My chest
Thaws out, expands in foaming desert heat.
My pores open like a fan. I sail along
Between sky and sand as if gliding on water.
Early wanderers here sailed in prairie schooners.
Are these extremes of sailing my immortality?
Whose graves are we passing? . . . Metal fields of death.
Old years, old shapes, lie hot in sun like cast-off,
Withering snake-skins. A billboard shines blackly:
"*Now Is The Time for Salvation. I. Cor.*"
A Christian country boils with urgency.
Is the time for salvation not eternal?
When the Buddha sat under the Bo Tree at Gaya
After seven years of meditation in the forests,
What he experienced was awakening, *bodhi*,
But he spoke only the deep language of silence.
We are entering Lovelock . . . Love-lock . . .
The Americans even name an isolated town
After their pounding problems of the heart.

V

My long, flat nose is fixed to the wind.
I have become a savage hunter, destroying insects.
My speed creates a vacuum trap for little wings
That sucks them in, smashes them to spots.
Speed, speed, at what pace comes the final unity,
The God-Head merging, bringing endless peace?
A man's flesh is so light, so fanciful,
How can he feel my solid roots, my heavy surge
Through air, my skin printed with quick, changing images?
Near Fallon, prideful signs announce the sale of
Hearts of Gold Canteloupes and Bronze Turkeys.
I savor a dry hunger that feeds on liquid energy

3

From red towers in bright stations with flags
And prizes for my feeding. When I stop,
Servants hurry to greet me in white uniforms,
Pat or *Jim* lettered on their pockets.
At Elko, steaming in ninety degree heat,
I feed beneath urgent proclamations to visit
The polar bear, the ten thousand dollar
Cowboy boots with jewels and rich leather.
Money is forced into long-handled machines.
Cylinders fly in circles, flash images of fruit.
A tense legend forms in sticky air.
Perhaps the polar bear is chosen to assume
The burden of heat, wear the rich boots of wealth,
Work the levers until the rolling cylinders clank,
Shine with waterfalls and pristine mountain grace.

VI

Sizzling along through endless level salt,
The Great Salt Desert, a shimmering salt world . . .
At Wendover, the statue of a green cowboy
Swaggers over the white. His plaster hat is
An enormous mushroom shield against the sun.
His sweet cow face smiles a boy's innocence.
Weapon of loneliness strapped around his waist,
He dreams to be an ancient warrior, not the youth of time.
My search through speed is like a jagged thunderbolt
As I pursue the white line to the horizon,
A line dividing the pursuer from his destiny.
What Karma might occur if I should swerve?
My bride may wait behind the spouting giants
That dominate our passage, as if whale-ghosts
Lose the ocean and turn to haunt the road.
I limp to their pounding, long for
A liquid, flowing dolphin-leaping.
This whale-ghost society surges with frenzy
Splitting time into quick, tearing explosions,
As the grace of Buddhist bells fades—

4

"The sound that frees us from
all agonies and sorrows . . ."
Desert and farmlands merge in evening glow.
MacPherson roars his exuberant laugh
At images of food staring like tamed miracles.
"Look!" he shouts, "How's that for a slogan?"
"FOR US THE IMPOSSIBLE TAKES A LITTLE LONGER,"
Is written in arrogant gold across a factory breast.
America's genius tames miracles to placid facts.
As they devour MacPherson's chocolate candies,
The children ask the meaning of "impossible,"
As if it were an invisible eye
Shining through clouds into the sun of vision.

VII

Desert cactus, signs, reflect on my glass forehead:
"Watch For Sleepy Drivers," "Patrolled By Airplane."
I am being watched . . . If I could only look up steadily,
Look back . . . The desert at night is a brilliant
Wilderness of stars, sapphire, diamond distances;
My gaze locks straight into the singular beams
Illuminating rocky soil until we stop in buildings
Guarded by gigantic plaster animals. An electric legend
Shines: *DINOSAUR MOTEL.* My family chatters in to sleep.
I rest, my hot parts cool, begin to shiver
In cold night air. Above me colored lightning tubes
Flash on the dinosaur shapes. *"Terrible lizards . . ."*
Those cold-blooded reptiles lived millions of years
Before the Buddha found his Noble Truths
Led to Nirvana. Some walked upright, some on
Four legs, some shaped wings for flying.
What died when their ponderous spirits disappeared?
Perhaps they too are changed to metal beings,
Their lumbering size and lost dreams of elegance
Forgotten memories smoldering in steel bodies
And glass eyes of speed. Around me, my chilled companions
Shine dully through dust in our waiting
Night positions. Hail, fellow Dinosaurs!

5

VIII

After fulfilling his private and public duties,
His obligations to family and the landscape of his birth,
The Buddha set forth on his task of contemplation
To enter the spiritual world,
To find "unexcelled, complete awakening."
He said farewell to his family, gave up his sexual needs,
Forsook his worldly body and goods . . .
But I am in the world again, I serve my family,
Yet cannot know the river of their beings.
MacPherson dreams of a new candy he will manufacture.
He speaks of a *Chocolate Tower* and a *Skyscraper Box*.
To manufacture a candy . . . With what softness
His machines must shine . . . If communion with my family
Flickers, lost, we possess each other to insure communication.
The laughing children hurl their waste into the air;
Their father calls them fondly, litterbugs . . .
As for my sexuality, I still desire.
When I pass attractive metal beings,
I stare at knobs, curves, lamps, sniff their bodies.
In our swift world, a family vision swells;
I must not lose the sense of marriage
For steel bodies wake, like sleeping flesh,
To different joys. If we are born metallically,
That birth too can flare forth in a Star of Fire.

IX

My family and their servant wander on,
Pursuing faint trails of American pilgrims.
We pound into a National Monument — The Badlands.
Tormented, cracked towers of crumbling rock
Shine through red vistas of volcanic eruptions.
Such beautiful, lonely violence! Why must I pray for peace
When the eternal lesson is violent revelation,
Contemplative suffering. "Suffering alone exists,
Not he who suffers," said the Buddha . . . We sway on.

Suddenly after bent, twisted desert forms
The land climbs green again, The Black Hills;
Trees and granite mountains mix graciously.
Enormous stone faces push the sky away
From the horizon! Awe-struck, MacPherson's wife
Whispers, "Mount Rushmore!" Hundreds of travelers
And their metal companions stare at ancient memories,
Giant presidential heads, Washington, Lincoln, Jefferson . . .
The twitching, energetic children question loudly,
"Who's hiding in the back with his mustache?"
MacPherson chuckles forth his answer:
"The man with the Big Stick, Theodore Roosevelt."
Oh blessed America, to reveal yourself so casually
In such gigantic images! You transform me
With your giant ways. This pilgrimage to size
Possesses me with sniffing power, the certainty
That I am an investigating FURY. We circle on
Through the gentle-flowing Black Hills, bounce
Slowly up a dirt road. Whoa! My low stance
Attracts the rocky earth. I suffer intimate pangs.
I ring with clanging sounds, choke with dust.
We stop. A blast of light, shattered stone
Splinters the sky! Who is attacking?
Another giant mountain cracks, emasculated
By dynamite. MacPherson grins and shouts:
"Get a load of that Crazy Horse Memorial."
Blow up the mountain to create an Indian Chief!
The Sphinx was only seventy feet high, the Pyramid
Of Gizeh a mere four hundred eighty-one feet;
Crazy Horse, his wild hair tossing in the wind,
Will conquer America from a record altitude
Of five hundred sixty-three feet! Redeem the rebel!
Carve the terrible story on the mountain
To mark injustice in granite letters three feet tall,
Betrayal, rape, massacre of the Indians,
The murder of Crazy Horse when he was only thirty-four:
". . . For us the past is in our hearts, the future
Never to be fulfilled . . . My lands are where my dead lie buried."

7

Is this what resurrection means, great memories
Of desecrated pasts? Or do we change anonymously,
Shape gliding into stronger shape we cannot perceive
Until the pure balance of necessity is achieved
And every gracious form of existence honored
By the acceptance of unique, changing individuality.
Oh Crazy Horse, your fate is that the saintly martyrs
Are never buried. They burst from mountains in flames
And ride eternal roads until they earn their peace.
Blessed be the name of Buddha who has given me
A smaller torment, a lesser wandering through fate.
Look out, MacPherson, stupid man! This curse,
Can't you feel my stopping powers are tired?

X

My aching soul revives . . . It is a long salvation . . .
I search on, I am changed again.
Cornered in the metal forest of an unknown city,
I crouch here gazing at fanciful, popular vistas,
Still seeking virtuous views. Around me circles
The alarm of sirens searching through dim streets.
I yearn to move again, but my family has forsaken
My wounded body. MacPherson, MacPherson, where are you?
What happened to us? Why could not our family roots bloom?
Above me flashes a bright-colored, glittering banner:
   "SAM HAS 'EM! COME AND GET 'EM!"
A white series of numbers is painted on my glass.
$750.00 . . . Is that the value of my new flesh?
I have been altered, re-created, colored in red flames.
My old parts accept with expectation their new
Mechanical companions. As in the beginning,
Strangers approach cautiously to touch me.
Yesterday a man liked me, felt me all over.
I shined at him. Perhaps we will wander together
And he will lead me to the fire of revelation:
   "Nirvana is, but no one seeking it;
      The path there is, but none who travel it . . ."
I am learning how to be a Buddhist car.

8

Buffalo Man

Looming large, enticing, swaying on gin,
She accused me at the party in the smog,
Attacking my too obvious guilt
As a minor bureaucrat, a small, resigned urban man.
"You must believe you are a buffalo.
Breathe correctly. Learn to lumber."
"It's tough to lumber when you're small,"
I pled, smiling my weak sophistication.
"Nonsense, don't be so defensive.
You must think you're large, awkward,
Even a little stupid at times,
Unmistakably present, a looming hulk
Of male existence. That will end your difficulties."
Well, I laughed and began our relationship.
Somehow she changed my life. I charge her now
With a definite, if ironic, dream of size,
Aware of my slaughtered skin and meat,
Surviving proudly in small enclosures,
My downtown office cubicle from which I break out at night.
Ready for treachery, aware of fences in my masquerade,
An obsolete, thickskinned animal with frontier eyes,
I endure with patience . . . I love . . .
Although I feel like a monument that moves,
She's given me a place, a mask in which to live.

Erwin Samsen at the Sin and Flesh Pond

Must we always be ruled by names?
Erwin James Shrewsbury Samsen I was named.
How could I walk to school in that decoration?
This pond seems only water, an average polluted shore,
But it is called the Sin and Flesh Pond.
How can we picnic at such a haunted place?
I am already aroused. Are you ready for dessert?
Across the way, the statistics of that hamburger stand:
"1,548,286 burgers served . . ."
It is some kind of amazing record,
This flesh eaten near the Sin and Flesh Pond.
In China restaurants are called in modesty,
"The Second-Class Establishment of Mr. Hsiang,"
"That Trifling Place in the West Market," or
"The Restaurant Into Which You Would Not Take A Dog."
Down the road a sign advertises Frito-Lay.
What penetrating names America creates
Near the Sin and Flesh Pond! Are you ready, my darling?
Flesh is the joy in which we lose our names.
Here at the Sin and Flesh Pond,
I reduce my name to Erwin Samsen and make love,
Make love against the names of my country.

Living in a Boxcar in San Francisco

When you get older, you kind of settle like a house,
Except in my case, it's a boxcar . . . Smoke down
The doubledeck freeway, take a quick look out your window
Before you hit the distance . . . You'll see me sticking up,
My big boxcar solid in backyard sun, challenging the freeway,
Fresh brown paint, white-lettered name on the side:
EL CABALLO, Spanish for horse, we used to go bumping
From ranch to ranch, endless grazing land, horses
Kicking against the boxcar walls, waiting to run . . .
When they started building the freeway, it took a lot
Of sitting to get my boxcar left smack at the end of the line
When they retired me along with the railroad's end.
They were bulldozing everything for the freeway, trees,
Hills, houses . . . You bet they didn't expect a boxcar!
You should have seen their eyes frost up when they looked
Down from their surveying gadgets and saw this silent
Old hulk of a witness watching them. How they screamed
Before they decided to go around a few yards
And leave me tight against the noise and smoke,
Their damn cars smashing all day and night.
So we go on. Not that it's a war. They don't pay me
No attention except they got to slow down for the curve.
I've had her fitted with lights and I sleep in her now.
I'm kind of deaf, so those cars pounding up there,
Going where they have to go, don't bother me.
I pull into my boxcar, my lights shining at the
End of the line, maybe the last brakeman of the old,
Clicking western rails, train whistling to the desert stars,
Slow puff over tough mountains to the waiting sea . . .
When there's a frontier to remember, you got to live in it.

The Jovial Mortician

When I met the jovial mortician
And asked his profession, he only grinned
And handed me his card with the inscription:
"I'm the last man to let you down."
Club-time, fraternal luncheon meeting,
Hour of buttonhole flowers, civic speeches,
Southern Fried Chicken, Mashed Potatoes,
Hot Rolls, Rocquefort Cheese Salad,
Vanilla Ice Cream, Cookies, Coffee . . .
Gradually, during the election of officers,
Just after the Merit Awards and charity
Exhortations, he loaded me with gifts:
Ballpoint pen, clubpin with a topless girl
Climbing out of a casket, floral bouquet
For my secretary's help with his mailing lists.
Enthusiastically, I undressed for the grave.
Lying there in my plush satin coffin,
My best blue suit radiantly pressed,
White carnation in my buttonhole,
Handkerchief triangled correctly
From my lapel pocket, I stared up
Through my painted, cosmetic face
To see him looking down, reassuring me
Of his gift as the master of metamorphosis.
"Relax," he smiles, "I've filled your veins
With the solid elixir of eternal life . . ."

The Columnist Listening to "You Know" in the Park

Listening, you know, to voices in the park,
I hear the great American gesture,
"You know," weaving through wandering words
Like the roots, you know, of a tree;
And I think, what is it, you know,
In twining words groping for meaning
That makes, you know, a connection,
You know, a spark, a surge of green,
Sometimes, you know, a kind of branching
And flowering, a tree of language,
And the whole damn tree stands there,
You know, like a sentinel, warning
The hell with communication! You know,
Say what you mean, but the meaning,
You know, is how you see and hear the tree.

Bouncing Vision of the Commuter

Far away from the threat of foreign countries
That we watch, supervise intimately on television,
Radio, with our secret communications,
We let the Old Stone Bank buy our homes for us,
Rise to solve the fast car that we must drive slowly,
The maze of roads on which we mark the gas stations,
Stores, and bars of our daily commuting.
Along the freeway, dedicated advertisements
Blare with subtlety, shine their miracles
Of goods and bads. An advertisement reader
In a forced career, I mark the pages
In my favorite magazines as they force my mind to dream.
Daily, the job to which I travel grows more remote,
Time on the trips becomes tighter, our cars demand
Superior servicing, construction crews loom
Massive in their giant machines and concrete monuments.
Tense at the destination, we drive underground
Or wait impatiently high in the air for departure.
As I am taught the role of a commuter,
I hum, rehearse my tunes on the journey—
How to whistle, sing, chirp, in my comfortable cage.

The Burning Watcher

The December storm briefly suspended,
Ice melting, still air alert for sound,
I burn papers on the lonely beach
Strewn with oil-soaked stones and garbage,
Oil companies leaking money on the shore.
Behind me, a watcher is watching me,
A fat, tough sea gull, a strutter,
His mouth clamped on a long silver fish.
Refusing to release his greed, he can't take off,
So he glares at me. To tease him,
I move closer, curiosity down the slide to scorn.
Clutching his fish, he waddles indignantly away,
Paddles through greasy water to a rock
Ten yards off shore to show his scorn
And preserve his meal, frustrated that
He can't fly, eat, and mock me from the air
At the same time. I almost throw a rock to scare him,
But restrain myself, spectator to his greed.
Forced to eat, he sucks the big fish down his throat
Like a vacuum pump turned high to emergency;
Then takes off, ringing the air with shrill anger,
Flying around me in a fury of joyous delight
At eating his fish and having his flight too.
After the burning I tell my wife about the gull's rage,
She shrugs: "You gave him indigestion . . . Was that nice?"
Eye-driven are the ways of burning watchers,
Who stare and find in visionary questions,
Enigmatic answers disguised as burning action.

The Game-Master Explains the Rules of the Game for Bombings

> "The signal is the thing."
> A Pentagon Official.

1

Begin in cockpit darkness,
the aim of secret instruments.
Security is locked space, walls nameless indoors,
a panel of superior pointers . . .
Begin with the shining of engineered rules.
Team-players, our radium-bright, clockwork fingers,
alter the sky to shine with brillance
at key terminals, decisive points,
as the automatic battlefield sparkles, blinks . . .

2

The enemy must be reminded
what the rules of the game are,
whether he understands them or not.

3

Whether he understands them
is not particularly important.
The signal is the thing.

4

When the grid sparkles, lights flash,
the bomb-bay opens like a metal eye
glinting with computed knowledge.
No player sees the earth any more.
The signal starts the run and drop.

5

After the clouds color with flame,
reconnaissance planes snap pinpoint photographs.
The specialist interpreters study
how to wind up the war
without nuclear escalation.
New signals are discovered
on the photographs . . .

6

Blown up in the print shop, the signals
are proved out into rules to protect
the sanctity of the demilitarized zone,
provide productive discussions
at the conference table,
fill up the credibility gap,
verify the body count.
Foreign languages are filled
with signal-pointers.

7

Files store the newly printed designs.
Manuals are written to instruct the rules.
Translators work on electronic codes.
On the ground, in the flesh,
The signal is the thing.

The Suicide Runner

"A good elbow shot broke my nose in Chicago.
Another guy rammed his fist in my neck
For the hell of it. You might as well
Get out of town if you worry about
Breakin' your nose . . ."
Cowboy boots propped on a chair,
Phone pressed to a scarred ear, the suicide runner
Grins into the plastic: "Look, darling, don't say
You'll call me Monday after the game.
Lord, don't ever say you'll call *after* a game.
I'll be gettin' drunk, bettin' at the race track,
Or lookin' for bail. When you're on a suicide team,
You don't wait till next week to start living.
Just get me those ringside seats will you, love?
Don't promise me nothing you can't produce."
Banging down the phone with a joyous "Yippee!"
He turns to the long-legged girl holding a fur coat.
"Put it on me, babe! I earned that. Hundred per cent
Timber wolf and cost me 750 bones. Great to go
Strutting in the snow. Wanta know something, sweetie?
Next punt I run back I'm gonna get *you* a coat . . .
I had to prove I was no rookie on the suicide team.
After my first game, we're in this bar, see,
And they send me for drinks 'cause I'm a greenie
In the suicide business. I go get six martinis.
Before I swing back to the table, I drink two.
Then I wait till the old guys drain their drinks;
I grab their glasses—and chew 'em up without
Spitting out a piece. 'Course I didn't eat
The real big pieces of glass or the long stems.
That's lookin' for trouble. But they kinda got
The idea I ain't afraid to be a suicide runner . . ."
Putting on his fur coat, he parades before her mini-dress.
"That's some thick wolf, honey. You know I dreamt
Of running back a kickoff in this fur through the snow.
Wouldn't that be great? Those bastards see a damn fur coat

18

Comin' at them, suddenly they think they're chasin' a wolf . . .
When I'm goin' full steam, you know, it's like bein' hit
By a motorcycle travelin' forty miles an hour.
Those white lines shake like a buffalo stampede
As a thousand pounds of trouble come crazy-doggin' you
To mess you up. See, dearie, why I dream of runnin'
In my fur coat, closin' my eyes, steppin' high like a bitch?"
He runs in his fur coat through the mirror.
"Let's get it straight, sweetie. You want a suicide runner,
You got me. I gotta live against all those tackles
Who get named Cannibal of the Week . . .
Before I hit camp last summer, I worked for free
On a garbage truck as a swamp rat. That's the sharp tooth
Jumps out and picks up all them heavy cans.
But I didn't just pick up that stinkin' garbage.
I *threw* it on the truck like I was flamin' mad.
I spent six weeks as a swamp rat and three days in jail
For what some eyeglasses lectured me was wild drivin' and stuff . . .
When you're a suicide runner, love, you're in the wilderness.
You've gotta yell, "I'm gone," and go for free out of the trap."

The Dramatic Poet Argues with the Lyric Poet

A blunt face and peering eye
Against your lofty, classical grace,
We stand here in conversation,
Two statues arguing the styles
Of different civilizations . . .
I praise those poets who talk
And you admire those who sing.
You say my trudging prose is
Quicksand for your dancing song.
You sing the classic, victorious lyre
Against my theft of lines
From taut, colloquial prose.
The artful cadence of your voice
Sings shadows out of silent dust,
Lyrics to haunt my plodding time—
Yet, through your graceful song,
My narrative is slowly heard,
My characters begin to live
Love's dialogue of action
Beyond the privacy of song.

Lookin' for Gas at the Youth Guidance Center

What kind of gas are you goin' to give me?
I like the sweet-smelling kind don't burn.
I want to go on a trip, man . . .
I smelled it once when I lived in
One of them ten foster homes
Where you paid them to keep me.
You paid 'em with those checks
Got holes in 'em. Some kind of smart-assed
Machine punches holes in hard green paper.
They used to show me those checks
When they bought me. When I goofed off
They shipped me back to your Youth Guidance Center . . .
You're the guide, man. I guess I'm the youth,
But I got no age. You won't let me wear even a little mascara
Till I'm eighteen. I think I'm sixteen.
It's a date on some paper. At night you lock me
In my room the way you locked your gas tanks
When I tried to drain out some of that good gas.
I don't know if I'm a boy or girl,
Though my breasts are big and I've got a cunt.
You don't want me to fool with the blinds
On the window. You watch me when I go to the bathroom.
I can't spell or read good,
But I know what I say most of the time.
I can't seem to do nothing right.
I want to fill up my mind with good gas
And take off . . . Zoom, man,
Guide the youth to the good gas.

Report from the Housewife to the Moving Company

WAS VAN CREW COURTEOUS?
    The mover walked out singing,
    "I never knew how much I loved you,
    I never knew how much I care," —
    Carrying a sofa on his head.
DID VAN CREW PRESENT A CREDITABLE APPEARANCE?
    The packers wore white coveralls
    Blazing your company's name stitched in Gothic red,
    A uniform appearance glowing with incredibility.
    The mover and his two helpers loomed seven feet tall
    Like football giants. Because of their muscle
    I could not discern unique identities
    Beneath the mountains of skin-ripples.
    Credibility vanished in tribute to moving.
WERE YOU PLEASED WITH SERVICE RENDERED?
    By evening, after they had moved
    The fifteen hundred pound marble table,
    The mover and his helpers dripped sweat.
    They were so tired they could only stagger,
    Curse at each other; they seemed hardly
    To understand the spirit of four-letter words.
    My furniture was smothered carefully in green blankets
    Which the mover unfolded from a weary distance
    As if he had forgotten the still roots of sitting.
    The service rendered was beyond pleasure.
WERE THERE ANY WORRIES IN CONNECTION
WITH YOUR MOVE?
    I remain a little worried about Reno and Ohio.
    Moving is a different space. The mover told me, "No one
    Can stand me for more than a few days at a time.
    My wife cut out on me. I go it alone now.
    I don't even like a helper to drive my truck.
    It's too tough to try and get along with him.
    That way, you have to take care of people.
    This way, steaming east, I stop in Reno,

Park my truck in an alley, hit the fast clubs
For a couple of days. Then I just keep steaming east,
Around Ohio, though . . . Last summer, speeding through,
I lost my sticker for that corn country."
WHAT SUGGESTIONS WOULD YOU OFFER
TO IMPROVE THE SERVICE?
Dear Sirs,
The question of improvement
Has, I'm afraid, no stationary solution.
I go on moving in the wind,
Watching the wind move
The insanity from moving.
May the morning
Discover the silent destination
Free from movement.

Boy Watching a Light-Bulb Death in a Country Town

Tight to an old man's shack
I smoke, watching his light
Burn speech into silence.
His bulb blazes just
Above his skinny reach,
Huge, round, a naked glow
Hung from a butcher's cord,
Some kind of execution show.

That stingy oldster, his messy house,
Make me shifty, angry,
I don't know how to help, just stare;
I watch his light-bulb death
Hating that lonely glare,
Knowing he lies invisible below
The glaze, sinking in sleep,
An old puzzle, stiffening slow.

One winter night, his long cord
Wavered, swung, cracked.
He lashed the light up and down
As though it were a whip
Attacking enemies in the town.
Somehow the bulb stayed weird
With light, flaring wildly through
Shadows that soared and disappeared.

When the light stopped swinging
And stood still, I wanted to hope,
"Maybe he's dead or blind at last.
It's just a light now
Burning up something past."
But I keep on watching the light,
Growing older in my room,
Learning a different kind of sight.

The Duck Watcher

To Edwin Honig

1

Slowly, through the fading leaves of the autumn beech,
a white ship . . . the opera commences . . .
Lohengrin riding his swan!
No, a plain boat in a polluted bay . . . Ducks floating . . .
What references can I summon magically
to be a T. S. Eliot of hidden knowledge?
Was there a duck somewhere in the Grail legend?
You are too small and squat to be a swan.
The gull easily outsoars you in power and grace.
I must learn how to see without legends.

2

They have taken to catching light!
Tricks of the sun, perhaps,
or is it that they turn and turn
        toward the light?

3

Winter stupidities . . . Hundreds of black ducks,
floating stoics in the cold wind,
ducking for invisible food,
their asses up in the air like comic flags.
This is what it means to endure . . .
I too am looking for invisible food,
my ass to the rear of time like any beast.

4

The ducks scrape the water, surface-precision.
Do not ignore the metaphor, they have a razor quality
of sharpness in their slash for food.
They open up inches of surface depth as they . . .
My god, that is why they are called *duck!*

25

5

Duck in the snow is like cork in a bottle,
pressed tight against that wet force . . .
Inaccurate vision. The cork is a cold agent
of tight preservation, the duck a warm spirit
of survival, he bounces, twists, glides
with the wind, absorbing the force of chance;
the duck is only like a cork, floating elements,
light forces in a world of heavy weights,
bobbing, weaving, Ariel touch on solid earth.
Look, I am weaving too, but I cannot duck.

6

So many of them, are they ever lonely?
They surround loneliness
as if it were the center of a circle,
always moving tighter together
until the invisible center of loneliness
is obscured, shifted to the shore
where my house, my species, watch, alone.

7

Incredible how they veer and swerve in wind patterns.
Arrows, lines, squares, even a cross!
All too symbolic, their patterns mock me with symbols.
A symbol is what a duck hoists you by.

8

"See ducks, Common Black . . ." *Anas rubripes tristis* . . .
How sad the sound of science, particularly lost Latin.
To be called Common Black is also dangerous,
a classification failing as blood identity.
Who is that Common Black Duck drifting there?

9

Storm! Blizzard! Fronting the rising wind,
they face the waves like Nevsky's troops
facing the rigid line of Teutonic Knights,
but without uniform disguise, this is no film;
they are only floating feathers against nature,
a natural huddle of defense . . . How my duck-poem
goes from menacing aggression to football
is an American sequence of power . . .
I salute you, defensive American ducks.

10

God damn, a grey day, they are gone . . .
From a high house, I look out on a glaze.
The Glaze! It may be my mind.
The levels of water confuse me with their emptiness.
I cannot see the invisible life, hunted and hunter.
The Glaze has abolished depth.
I want to navigate backwards, forwards,
escape this dead center of the Glaze
that fixes the picture, kills time,
stops the heartbeat, pacifies even death.

11

Through the winter tree, the tanker approaches
as wind whips up the spindrift. Vacation boys,
full of assassin blood, fire beebie guns.
The ducks fly away. The tanker lingers,
its green forecastle bulging over a gut of oil,
steaming slowly away for heat and money.

12

They are floating in the juice of spring,
Black Dots of Memory . . .
I must leave this rented house

and my duck observations
before my vision dips completely duck.
Anas rubripes tristis . . .
The ducks are gone, they're changing
into Common Black Dots of Memory
as spring shatters earth with the old forms . . .
I am what is around me, said Stevens,
skin-possession, separation inside,
the observer struggling for an eye of wonder
to create from those lost black ducks
The Uncommon Black Dots of Memory . . .

Confidential Data on the Loyalty Investigation of Herbert Ashenfoot

Until the birth of my thirtieth birthday
I sailed the wide harbors of illusion,
Wind and war of parents over my silent head
While the bell of identity tinkled
At my window like the Good Humor salesman.
Around me the black armies like bats
Lay darkly in their caves of caution
And for Security I joined the Civil Service.
Rating P-3, almost a pristine pursuit plane,
I roared from basket in to basket out
And all my days were clocked and carefree.
At the dawn of thirty my reform began.
My loyalty was cleaned and prodded
And my dreams divorced from all emergencies.
Propped at my desk by aspirin, I typed
Like a hermit crab in the tears of my time.

A Guilty Father to His Daughter

Why are you always glad to me?
Shouts my daughter gladfully
A twist of time a tuneful word
Happy I roll into the glad gully

High father in my Morning Glory
Silk virtue violently in me
I rule my family like an old fox hound
And father my way in fancy

When I curse her she catcalls
And cancels her sparky consent
Carnal her sun foams out and her flesh
Firms between us fixed as cement

Prince of Fathers in my glad gully
Hobbledehoy in my fatherly rain
Why are you always glad to me?
Demon down the fatherly drain.

Fabre, The Bughunter

Only an exile, a Japanese
In France, would cry Banzai to the Bughunters;
Certainly not the French ladies with green thumbs—
    Bugbear, object of dread,
Bugaboo crawls imaginary terror in the dark—
Words from bugs disdained and giddy bughunters,
    Queer men with nets and jars.

    A country bumpkin;
His parents fed him by setting fire to heath and
Gorse, where ashes nourished oats and potatoes.
    At the age of six
He asked himself: "How do I perceive light?"
He shut his eyes: darkness; opened them: light;
    The simple sense of vision.

    Soon a love of Latin
From Vergil's web-fingered tales of bees and crows,
Cicadas humming, the turtle dove and nanny goat.
    Born to teach,
He sat as Master behind a desk and for relief
Peered inside at wasps' stings, beetles' wing casings
    And snapdragons' seed vessels.

    One sweet-smelling spring day,
Teaching his class Practical Surveying by stakes and tangents,
Boys disappeared after a big, black, solitary bee.
    Fabre disappeared too,
Into his imagination, a world of thyme honey
Where history was weatherbeaten and natural if you earned
    The title of Great Observer.

    Paris was hell.
Forced there finally to receive the Legion of Honor,
He stammered and called the third Emperor Napoleon, 'Monsieur.'

Driven at last from Avignon
By the old ladies who couldn't bear his teaching
Young girls why a man breathes, how to plant flowers and seeds,
    And similar subjects.

History is indignant,
But Fabre was a good seed-planter himself, eight children
And two wives who knew enough to let the dead birds
    Rot on his study table.
Everything seemed over, he was seventy-four years old,
Some fame, writer of a few celebrated monographs,
    But a seedy reputation.

Then to Sérignan.
'The Eden of Bliss,' he called it. 'This accursed ground
Which no one would have as a gift is an earthly paradise
    For the bees and wasps.'
He grew weeds. Thistles thrived with their prickly
Stems and leaves, and their tough, cylindrical heads
    Like heavy hammers.

Couch grass too,
With roots creeping through the snapping smudge
Of all wild plants reckless in their wild sense,
    Thus called weeds.
He watched and wrote: 'Here come the hunters,
Carpenters boring wood, architects in pasteboard,
    Builders of clay,

Collectors of leaf-pieces,
Plasterers mixing mortars, workers in gold-beaters' skin . . .
The promptings of instinct in its highest manifestation.'
    Lived until ninety-two,
The last eighteen years at Sérignan, in seclusion,
Famous and lonely, his family dead and dispersed, while the
    Frogs yacked May into his pond.

To the hermit of Sérignan,
Writing for the young whom he wished to love Natural History,
Who said to the technicians: 'You rip open the little creatures,
　　　But I cause them to be loved;
You work in a chamber of torture and dismemberment,
But I observe under the blue sky,'—this Banzai
　　　From a Japanese in France.

Seurat

Degas called him 'The Notary.'
  Dressed in black suits,
    Severe top hat,
      Pressed creases.

His only portrait shows his mistress.
  She sits in décolleté preening,
    Buxom as a barrel, and we know
      He loved her flesh.

Critics crawled on knees to mock his shimmering points,
  Smeared him with the label, 'Pointillism,'
    A wax-work, scientific painter;
      Jeered his dots as colored fleas.

But at the Grande Jatte, sunlit still every Sunday summer afternoon,
  Mental masters lean on formal canes like curios,
    And light gathers lemon-yellow lazily, where on
      Gentle grass glide the parasol ladies.

Neighbors

        Next door
In a shingle-sliding house,
With paint curling off like worms
        In their crawling pace,
Lives the neighbor whose guts I hate
        With his miser-face.

        His house
Is a jungle of mice and junk,
And he means to cut my property value
        With his ugly mess
Of broken furniture, decaying wood,
        Nothing to bless.

        In the morning
He stakes out his property line
With a tall, imaginary fence;
        I feel barbed wire,
Though he only hammers sticks in the ground
        With eyes of fire.

        His little head
Sits on his neck like a grape,
And the rags of his clothes fill with dirt.
        To treat him mean
I give laughing parties for my friends;
        He watches behind a screen.

        I think he was born
To live a hermit's isolation
And serve himself with trembling hands,
        Trapped in a shell
Of darkness where cold air blows
        No saving church bell.

But every time
I look at him with hate he changes,
His shoulders sag, his head sinks,
    He decays with his house,
As I paint desperately to keep my house alive
    And set traps for any mouse.

The Old Woman and the Cat

White hair spiky in wind like wheat,
Deep, loamy eyes set in a dried-out skin,
She lifts the full bell of her skirt
And out pops a cat like a bursting balloon.
"I'm pushing ninety," she says with a push,
"I got that old cat down by the road.
He was slung up on a tree like a can
By a truck making time for the city.
His pelvis or something was broke
And that's why his stomach hangs down."
As she speaks, she feeds him a sandwich
And scraps of fish smell up the porch.
"I never saw a cat so round," I say,
"You sure it's only a broken pelvis?"
"Yeah, I can't stand that damn, busted cat.
Last winter rain poured through the roof
And I set out plates to catch the water.
There's nothing to do in this sleepy town,
But watch that cat lap water up
And gorge himself until he dies."
With a muttering quiver, she walks in the house,
And comes back with two cans of cat food.
"I'm not staying another winter," she says,
"It rains too much for an old woman here.
In the city I could ride around on a bus
And talk to people on the telephone
Instead of watching this busted, old cat."
She scoops out food with a blue veined hand,
Stoking the cat's impatient greed; his tongue
Licks out, and his yellow eyes shine
As his bloated belly sags on the floor.

The Newsboy Enters the Bar

"Hey, Newsboy!" call the evening patrons,
Sipping their drinks at the polished bar.
Green-tinted glasses over his blinking eyes,
He squints down the bar in dim light
And barks at all the grinning patrons.
The first bark brings out tittering jokes,
Laughter of recognition at the dog-boy
In his cracked shoes and baseball jacket.
But the second bark begins a silence:
This is a gray-haired man, not a dog.
Black headlines on the papers that he waves
Read: "ROCKET SOARS INTO THE MOON."
He barks, and the customers buy,
Twitching uneasily, the laughter lost.
At last he barks and no one buys.
A salesman on his stool bends over his gin,
The tattooed bartender wipes at glasses,
A thick-chinned blonde toys with a swizzle stick.
Barking defiantly, the old newsboy departs
Through swinging doors that shut on faded faces,
Silent, thinking of rockets soaring to the moon,
And the barking mind with which man soars.

The Scientist Observes the Protozoa

To The Achievements of Roman Vishniac

Under the moulding miracle of this microscope,
The commonplace curiously becomes magnificent;
Observe—here creeps a cautious little creature
Forever peering through the inch of his landscape;
There, a second who searches fixedly for food
Like a fat man always in fancy of famine.
Look! This tiny animal is called a floscularia,
So beautiful I name her Queen of the Microcosmos.
Long, fine hairs stream singularly from her head,
Contracting, expanding through rays of radiance.
Hers is the eternal hair of Helen, the hanging
Harvest of a beauty that attracts only victims.
A sudden shock and twisting shakes her body
When some animal approaches to explore her hair . . .
The shining strands fire into a menacing corona
That pushes the prey delicately into her body . . .
In muddy water, unseen, crawls an animal world
That has outlived the fifty thousand years of man
By half a billion years; before and beyond the
Blasting age of atoms, they reproduce their world
Of miniature conquest by radiant fission.

A Story of Soutine

Soutine the Sour,
Kindled by Rembrandt's "Woman Bathing,"
Searched for a country model, and at last
Found a peasant woman working in a field,
Her shovel feet bare in the dust.

When he prodded her
To pose, she thought him a snatchy lecher
Until she sensed the mystery of a man
Who had painted only one nervous nude;
Then she thought him mad.

But persuaded by pay,
Clumped bare-footed into the brook,
Skirt held up by her brick-red hands,
Staring at old chucklehead, the painter,
The fury of his cozening face.

For days he slaved,
Commanding the cloddish, fleshly shape
To flow fiercely in colors on the canvas.
Then one afternoon, crooked cumulus clouds
Gathered for a grimace of rain.

The peasant woman cried
For permission to run from her ponderous pose,
But he shouted at the cramps of her shivering body,
"Stand still!"—or she would be shocked by God
For the ruined work.

Through the riddling rain,
Thunder clapped and rammed into the driving darkness,
But Soutine painted on with the acid of vision.
At last the paint subsided, and his wilful eyes
Woke in the dark of his dream-land.

Blue and blubbering in the
Brook, the sodden peasant woman howled hysterically,
And from the rain-wet, singing surge of its colors,
The painting stared at her mortal behavior, reflecting
The arrogant mirror of art.

The Warrior at the Potlatch

"We fight our guests with property"
A Kwakiutl Indian Chief

Silent in splendor,
I march to the festival,
dangling ermine from my carved wooden hat,
sea lion bristles hanging from my catch . . .
See my ceremonial staff,
raven perched on a killer whale—
Big Hunter comes to the potlatch.

I gorge from this deep trencher,
carved by my host from a tree
shaped like a body fourteen feet long,
painted full-flowingly black and red;
I feast on four fiery courses,
fish oil broiling fresh sea food
from knees, belly, and head.

Glaring, we eat with fierce pride;
I fling scraps to the waiting dogs;
we begin the magic visions, weaving our tales,
the many otters killed with a backhand blow . . .
At last my host, the master
of cunning games, rises in majesty
to grant the gifts of woe.

Placid squaws, devilfish children,
even warriors who walked as friends,
have whittled for weeks at spruce and cedar;
they've carved totems, burnished canoe-bark,
woven fine goat-woolen blankets—
yet each gift they give me is
a trap-gift, a sentence to work.

I say goodbye to my days of pleasure,
since I must return two gifts for one.
My wandering warrior hands writhe in the trap of toil
where weakskinned painters polish presents with a curse.
I must labor with a woman's patience
shaping her little artificial gifts;
I am condemned to be a gift-nurse.

The Connoisseur's History of the Bathroom

My bathroom has a fireplace of white brick,
Sliding glass walls and a carpeted floor.
I live there in seclusion like a sybaritic hermit.
Outside the glass walls open on a terrace.
As I sit in my black terazzo tub, I watch
Luxuriant plants grow behind the dressing table,
And remember other familiar, classical bathrooms:
The Greeks and Romans thought of the bath as festival,
A center of sublime conversation, the rejuvenated spirit,
A leisurely scraping and steaming in the public baths
Provided by thoughtful tyrants. Christianity taught
Man was sinful if he removed his heavy clothes,
Hence scorn of the bath as Satan's lurking temptor,
And hiding of that room in shadows of necessity.
Believers in ornamentation and aromatic elegance of baths,
The lush, invading Moors horrified the Spaniards.
By the 18th century, the bath was "convertible,"
Disguised as a *chaise longue* for the aristocracy,
But a queen had private privileges:
> Marie Antoinette's bath, wrote Mary Gray Humphries,
> Had a tub room paneled in marble, "fed by swans
> Whose necks and heads are of silver." Behind the tub was
> A mirror "painted over with lovers
> Pelting each other with flowers . . .
> Mirrors were set in the ceilings, like crystal lakes
> Upside down amid garlands of flowers."
Plumbing in the 19th century brought new elegance.
Scarcely was there a workable toilet; instead,
A sculptured, porcelain dolphin held a conveniently shaped
Shell in its teeth. Petals and roses gilded the washbasin.
Bathtubs were housed in copies of period furniture.
The century turned to progress. In 1903, the *Woman's Book*
Said proudly: "The exposed tub and exposed plumbing
All make for health and cleanliness." Happiness too,
The concealment resolved, bathrooms turning to health rooms.
By 1908, the Statler Hotel in Buffalo advertised:

"A BED AND A BATH FOR A DOLLAR AND A HALF."
The modern tendency is back toward the elegant bath,
Glass-enclosed tub in gray mosaic tile, radiant heat
In the floor, towel ladder and handsome wall boards.
Usually, it is men who insist on ornate bathrooms.
A terrifying thought: the bathroom has replaced women.
My bathroom designer says, "People are mad for cherubs,"
And so I have them on the wall next to the counter basin
With foot pedals instead of faucets, which leave my hands
Free to pluck at gay towels. My clothes hang
From a hook inspired by a twitching peacock's tail.
My melon taffeta shower curtain guards the floor
And the mirror walls are lit with incandescent bulbs.
I think of an old jingle:
   "Come into the bathroom, Maud,
    The plumbing Cranes have built.
    There let us carouse with guilt.
    Come into the bathroom, Maud."
My wallpapers tend towards the mildly naughty.
This is the place where I forget I must wear clothes,
And nakedness shines across the room with its lost grace.

The Frozen Ink of Francois Villon

'Dried up and black as a baker's mop,'
So he described himself as the ink froze.
Done with the Bishop blessing streets,
Done with the girls, taverns, and thieves,
Done with the powerful operator of picklocks,
Done with Margot, bloated as a dunghill beetle
(We both love filth and filth runs after us),
Done with the cymbals, the lute, and the dice,
He stared at the ink frozen on the table.

'That man is lucky who has nothing.
I have my luck, I have my frozen ink.
I was born in the year that Joan was burned.
Child of poverty, I heard the hungry wolves
Prowl through Paris to kill women and children.
For a man who's poor, the high mountains
Will move neither back nor forth. They tower
Over the roaches that move in sour milk,
As I stare at the ink frozen on the table.'

'Where are the snows of the past? They are here.
I am sentenced to leave Paris for ten years.
Tortured, starved, chained, I am free to die;
Even princes have a destiny of death,
Yet I think of towns with the gift of hope.'
Fleeing Paris and the poor for his death,
He left the frozen ink in the room
And disappeared into January snow.
Slowly, the ink unfroze on the table.

Milton: The Puritan's Sword of God

Crack the five-beat rhythm, force it down,
Hard in the air, syllables harsh and heavy,
Satan does not kneel to regularity.
Rime is the invention of a barbarous age,
To set off wretched matter and lame Meeter.
Seek ancient liberty that the Heroic Poem speak:
God is a sword, the blade of blazing justice,
Plainness and brightness the essence of His truth,
As Cromwell shines through perilous battle
And rears God's trophies on the neck of Fortune.

> *Warr then, Warr*
> *Open or understood must be resolv'd.*
> *He spake: and to confirm his words, out-flew*
> *Millions of flaming swords, drawn from the thighs*
> *Of mighty Cherubim.*

Drawn from angels, the sword of War is
Glory, to live on the cutting edge of joy,
Where the true self is master of salvation
Under God's providence; the sword
Leaps out in fire when the Dogs of Hell advance
Under disguise of Custom and Authority,
The simple sword of reason, then, of poetry,
Slashing at webs of Custom, clearing light
And liberty, the best school of virtue.
Yet after the war between Heaven and Hell,
Before death, when eternal wrath burns
A path to the bottomless pit of devils,
And age tears the light away from eyes,
Who can seize the sword of simplicity?
The sword strikes into the mind, cuts here,
Cuts there; in conscience suddenly confused,
Blind Fury comes to slit the thin-spun life.

Descartes Composes a Ballet

Death looks like my natural daughter
Who died at the age of five; she dances
Toward me in her skeleton . . . I cannot remember
Her mother, though, long ago, it was a warm embrace.
Cold of death here in Stockholm . . . I rise
At five every morning to teach Queen Christina
In her study. She is killing me with arguments
Of how to live happily in sight of God and man . . .
Always I yearned for morning hours in bed
And warmth for thought. In the Bavarian Army,
During the Thirty Years War, I climbed in a stove
Each ice-shattered morning to keep warm
And meditate . . . The Queen is my stove,
Impatient youth, commanding mistress of logic.
With her I have analyzed love, and the Passions
Of the Soul residing in the tiny pineal gland.
Her Majesty of Argument has set me to compose a ballet . . .
Scepticism dances toward my luring senses.
Am I sitting by this fire in my dressing gown?
Sometimes I dream I sit here quietly for warmth
When I am naked in bed. Madmen have such dreams,
But there remains something I cannot doubt.
No demon can deceive me if I do not exist.
Though I think everything false, I am
Something since I think . . .
Small defense against this passionate Queen
Who walks in logical snow to freeze my age . . .
I have delved in matter and freed its substance
From the ancient world, if not from God.
Mind and matter are God's creatures, His will,
And hence distinct from Him. They dance
A singular science for which I went
On pilgrimage to the Blessed Virgin's shrine . . .
The dancers shall whirl in passion of faith
Out of the sun-lit south into this dark north . . .

God, being good, will not deceive their limbs.
If they stumble, it is her whirling will,
Her will to death that kills me in this cold land . . .
Even if mind sleeps in my daughter and madmen,
God's mind will dance in this ballet
And the Queen see my dancers triumph over death . . .
Why should we marvel if the light reflected
From the body of a wolf into the eyes of sheep
Excites them to quick flight? Mind is music,
God is beyond, God stands to Himself,
Invisible dancer who dances quicksilver vision.

Rousseau Takes His Five Natural Children
to the Foundling Hospital

1

I search for a man in the integrity of Nature,
And this man shall be myself. I know my heart
And have studied mankind. Such as I was,
I declare myself, sometimes vile and despicable;
At other times, virtuous, generous, and sublime.

My birth cost my mother her life
And was the first of my misfortunes.
Of all the gifts which Heaven gave my parents,
Only a feeling heart descended to me.
I wandered in Nature to feel the bliss of God.

2

My mistress was a needlewoman of good family.
Always a friend to decency in manners
And conversation, I took her part.
She saw in me an honest man, and I perceived
In her a simple heart, devoid of coquetry.

At first amusement was my only object;
Then, I found that I had given myself a companion.
I began by declaring to her shyness
That I would never abandon or marry her,
And so, we began to conceive bastards.

3

Too sincere and haughty in my inquiring mind,
I had to examine the destiny of my children
According to the laws of Nature, Justice, and Reason,
And those of that Religion, holy and eternal,
Which men have polluted with purest desire.

I trembled to entrust them to their mother's family,
Ill brought up, to be still worse educated.
In abondoning my children to public education
For want of the means of bringing them up,
I considered myself a member of the Republic of Plato.

4

Sometimes, in the privacy of my study,
With my hands pressed tight over my eyes,
Or in the darkness of the night,
I think that there is no God.
But I see the rising of the Sun,

As it scatters mists that cover the earth
And lays bare the wondrous, glittering
Scene of Nature; my clouded soul clears,
I find my faith again, and my God,
And I prostrate myself in His natural world.

5

I have written the truth; whoever examines my character
And pronounces me dishonest, deserves the gibbet.
The noble, savage man, when he has dined
Is at peace with all Nature; natural,
We sense the glad mystery of God.

Only by institutions is man made bad,
Yet that is my fear of the Foundling Hospital.
The faces of my children I have never known
Flare behind the walls of that grey school
And I see them, forever, at their education.

Freud: Dying in London, He Recalls the Smoke of His Cigar Beginning to Sing

"Double flesh,
 Double way;
   Love is a bed
 Where angel-devils
 Lash and play.

"Double warmth,
 Double flame,
   Love is the fury
 To love and find
 A single name."

In the smoke of my cigars, twenty a day,
I searched the roots of man's desire;
To bed at one in the morning
Until the smoke began to sing.
I enjoyed my food, my meat,
In a city whose name I have forgotten.
Rooted in one house for forty-seven years,
I analyzed and wrote and watched six children
Until the Nazis marched and the booted Commissar
Asked me to sign a statement of gentle handling.
I insisted on adding the sentence:
"I can heartily recommend the Gestapo to anyone."

The cancer grows in my jaw like a separate life.
Krebs, meaning cancer and crabs; strange that I
Who am fond of crabs should suffer from cancer.
A broadcast says: *This is the last war.*
Anyhow, it is my last war. The radium begins
To eat in and my world is what it was before—
An island of pain floating on a sea of indifference.
The stench . . . when my chow is brought to visit me,
She shrinks into a corner of the room.
I spend my hours lying near my study window

52

Gazing at my flowers in the garden,
My superb almond tree, its pink blossoms
Pouring beauty into the darkening world.
I never believed in a supernatural life;
This world of nature embraces everything.
Why, then, do I dream of religion,
And write of Moses in my final hours?
Man's helplessness remains, his father-longing.
The gods retain their three-fold task:
To exorcise the terrors of nature;
To reconcile the cruelty of death;
To make amends for all suffering and hate
The communal life of culture imposes on man.
In early centuries, men projected the Devil;
Today, their guilt turns in to physical pain.
Jews write to beg me not to tear from Moses,
In time of need, the legend of a Jewish hero;
But the truth must be sought. Moses blazes
In my imagination more than any other leader.
For three lonely September weeks in 1913,
I stood every day by Michelangelo's statue,
Studying it, measuring it, sketching it,
Until I captured the understanding for it:
Moses, angry at the dance of lust,
The sexual fury around the Golden Calf,
But mastering his passion for his cause,
Protecting the Tables of the Law.
It is so logical. Moses was an Egyptian Prince,
Not a Jew; Moses was the God who chose the Jews,
Desiring to make them equal to Egyptians,
To give them one God of purity and power;
And so he marked them with the rite of circumcision
And led them out into a land of freedom.
In the end, he was murdered in rebellion
And that murder bred the hope for a Messiah
Of retribution. Christianity, the son-religion,
Replaced the ancient, Mosaic, father-religion.

53

The little, Egyptian statues on my desk begin to speak:
God, the Father, always walks on earth
Until his sons unite to slay him.
What was it that surrealist artist said?
My cranium is reminiscent of a snail . . .
I crawled slowly through the years
Until the smoke of my cigar began to sing.
It is useless to go on . . . Burn me,
Place my ashes in a Grecian urn . . .

"Double-flesh,
Double-way;
   Love is a bed
Where angel-devils
Lash and play.

"Double-warmth,
Double-flame,
   Love is the fury
To love and find
A single name."

The Portrait of Gongora Speaks

He's painted me
As if I glare from a desert cave,
Enduring the poison of poetry . . .
My bald head bulges,
My sharp, scimitar mouth
Hovers over the quill-pen.
The pen is a dart,
The target invisible . . .
When it strikes,
The poison flows
A target so precise,
The poison flows to praise.

The Runner Finds His Immobility

Through soft snow, the white world melting,
I run trailing my shadow, a black kite.
Flying over snow is my high, am I a running machine?
My heart's a mysterious pump, I can hear it
Feeding my legs as I pound through cold,
Yet I'm running away from time, caught in a race
Before they closed the doors and invented machines.
If they're going to confine me, they'll have to
Catch me first, teach me about pumps and time.
Though my feet hit a little water
I skim the surface with my stride.
The secret is in the floating . . .
If you follow the air, you don't have to stop.
Only my toes tell me something is down there
That can't be earth, it's hard as glass.
When landscapes reel ahead, the forward motion,
The beauty of running is you can't go back,
There's no rear view, no rage to return to.
Running is a way to escape from revolt.
When I stop, I'm wet to my bones
From some deep world that is gathering.
This stationary act is too quiet.
My face is reflected in a prism
That disappears underground, a hidden mirror
Reflecting the absence of time.
That glitter fastens me in place, makes me descend.
My feet seem to be freezing in my shoes.
It's invisible down where my body sinks.
What is this, some new kind of waiting?
Look at me enclosed in ice.
Someone is teaching me a lesson about running.
I'll never learn it, I'll run again
Even if I have to find my feet, my shoes.
If I can never run, it doesn't mean I'm dead.
Maybe I deserve this immobility.

The Executive at Fifty

At the age of fifty, jaggedly,
I emerge on every giveaway list—
WIN TWO BEAUTIFUL HOMES OR $77,777.00—
(If seven were my number I'd spin a seventy dream).
SAVE THE CHILDREN! I have two and a half to save
And a wife locked into my insurance security.
The mail floods in, third class, my name
Written on glittering, imaginary checks—
HOW WOULD YOU LIKE A TRIP TO THE MOON OR
SETTLE TEMPORARILY FOR A WORLD GLAMOUR TOUR—
Still my wife is a formidable if complacent cook.
Nobody can tell me that a pecan pie
Ever did anything wrong in life
Even though it's my dream more than my appetite.
When that mail slaps in the box in the morning,
It's good to feel you're on the giveaway list
In one fatal swoop. Spend a large life
Driving upwards, lucky, tough in competition,
Commuting long distance, working out problems
That probe you like a turtle into your shell.
You're on the edge, medium high toward the top,
You've got a splitlevel house with plenty of room,
Appliances so bright they polish your eyes
In a suburb so neat the dirt can't get in—
And then the giveaway lists begin to arrive—
THE WORLD'S A WONDER IF YOU OWN YOUR PIECE
GET THE PERFECT PRIZE WITH THIS LITTLE COUPON—
I've got my pen. I'm printing my coupons perfectly.
Through bi-focal glasses I scan the small print for clues.
One day I'll win, then I'll be off.
Play it back again . . . The planet's a giveaway place
If you spin through survival and hit the list.

Karl Barth's Dream of Mozart

(For years, each morning before work on his Protestant
theological studies, Karl Barth played Mozart, seduced
by that *eros*. One night, tossing and tossed in his bed,
Barth dreamt that he was appointed to examine Mozart in
theology.)

A Baroque mockingbird, the little figure
Perched on my bed and sang,
Although his lips never moved.
I wanted to make the examination favorable,
Yet his music would never stop playing . . .
It is a child, if a divine child, in Mozart's music.
Only a child could have said scornfully:
"Protestantism is all in the head.
Protestants do not know the meaning
Of *Agnus Dei qui tollis peccata mundi."*
A child playing in Catholic, sensuous flesh,
Creating with genius a sophisticated innocence.
Absurd . . . How can innocence wear such sophistication?
I quizzed him gently, humorously, on his Masses.
There, I was in safe sound, away from the seductive guile
Of his charming women, Blonde, Dorabella, Pamina, Susanna . . .
My dear Mozart, we begin . . . *Please, do not smile or sing*
To distract me . . . In your 1779 Coronation Mass,
Scholars often point out that the soprano solo
Of the "Agnus Dei" foreshadows the sexual pulse
Of "Dove Sono," The Countess's love aria in *Figaro.*
Is this your true lamb of God? . . . *No answer* . . .
Please, gentle Sir, pay attention to my words . . .
You cannot always caress language with melody
And turn the lamb of God into a sensuous woman.
Claim for defense the *Musical Discourse* of Johann Bähr:
"May not the communicant be full of devotion
Though he is splendidly attired?" . . .
No one denies your devotion, my dear Mozart,

But your tone, the twist, glitter of your attire,
Has not your lamb an excessively liquid, female touch? . . .
Silence . . . That never-ending music . . .
I hesitate, Sir, to mention the temptations
Of your nocturnal club, its unknown rituals,
Freemasonry, that period when you wrote
Nothing for the church and succumbed
Totally to the enticement of Masonic rites.
You transformed them into fleshly, sensuous cadences
That sacrifice religion to the lover's touch . . .
Stop singing to me . . . The examination is over.
You fail, you have refused to speak.
Every morning before I study the hard words of revelation,
Why am I condemned to your *eros*,
To the seduction of your melodic love?
Does the savior's flesh dance from his grave
To marry every doubter to his doubt?

The Graffiti Fingers of the Theology Student

Deep in the skins of graffiti,
As deadbeats pass from bar to can,
I read on the chipped wall:
    "God Is Dead"—Nietzsche
Underneath, some cripple has scribbled:
    "Nietzsche Is Dead"—God
Another lost graffiti artist
Has drawn a picture of God naked,
Dirty hippie beard, long hair,
Drifting bell-like tongue
Where archaic wonders, Greek, Latin,
Hebrew, ring in silent majesty . . .
Two layers up, a rocket soars
In lift-off of space visions,
Overkill, afterburner, doomsday tape,
Escalation, go-reflex for megadeath . . .
I drew the hippie God. I drew the rocket.
I am the digger for pornographic signs,
Cutting out the death of Nietzsche,
Celebrating the death of God.
Something is growing into me, roots
Cracking through the city's walled-in poverty.
Driven out by doubt, I walk at night
Seeking to lose the sky in grey districts.
I stumble over the discarded drunks
Before they're tossed into the wagon
For their evening log-pile ride to jail.
I put my hand on the thighs of whores.
I fight off the cripples on crutches
Blocking my way, demanding money,
Indignant at my gift of pennies,
And end up at this drifter's bar
With whores, thieves, eyes looking for a fix,
Where wounds flow out of the wood,
Carved mockingly in the walls.
"The enormity of evil is crushing me,"

Tolstoy said, "driving me to doubt everything."
But evil is still brilliant to me,
Floating in its haze like an eerie cloud.
I have not learned the heavy weight of doubt.
I am still searching for the Church of Freedom
And all the ministers seem prisoners to me.
When I learn to read everything in the graffiti,
My fingers will start their automatic writing,
The roots of doubt will shoot through them in fire,
The great, sacrificial handwriting of blood
Will shine in a new language on the wall.

The Pet Store Owner, His Parakeet, and the Encounter with Sarah Louise Burkett

I

When you keep parakeets for sale, you cage
A tiny flight you have to know how to catch.
When they get loose you run like hell after smallness
As if you were chasing a wrinkle in a lake.
Everything large chases everything small.
You learn to sprint with your net aloft
Like a charging flag, but that little bird
Perfects his vanishing act in space,
Flicks out of the shop into fog, traffic,
Me after him, crazy pursuit like a silent film.
Everyone jerks to watch, necks crane, feet
Tiptoe . . . Bodies angle . . . Swoop, the parakeet
Lands on a butcher shop bright awning:
FRESH MEATS FOR SALE . . . You wouldn't believe . . .
The damn bird disappears . . . The traffic stops,
Staring at me and my Sherlock Holmes net.
Whoever heard of hunting birds in a city?
A hundred invisible songs sing to me above the cars . . .

II

Next morning, fog-bound in my store, I get a call:
"My name is Sarah Louise Burkett . . ." What do I say?
"Yes, Ma'am. My name is Ralph Waldo Emerson . . ."
"Have you lost a parakeet?" The aged voice accuses me
Of carelessness by the control of tight syllables,
Old maid who makes life bend to the proper punctuation.
"Young man, can you identify your bird?"
My fifty years are so young I can't talk . . .
"Well, he's kind of . . . kind of little . . . a parakeet you know . . ."
Everything large is watching everything small . . .

"*That is hardly a description, young man.*"
"Sorry, description is not my bag of birds, lady."
"*You should take better care of your parakeet.*
Do you know I rescued him from great danger?"
"Ma'am, you're a hero." "*Heroine, Sir.*"
"Sorry, Ma'am . . . Where'd you find him?"
"*In that dreadful butcher shop, poor thing,*
Unable to fly . . . I had to crawl in on my hands and knees."
"You crawled in where?" "*I was forced to crawl,*
No one else seemed to know how to catch a bird.
How much is the parakeet worth to you, young man?"
Visions of eternal pursuit . . . Money as crawling reward . . .
"About a dollar I guess . . . You name a price, Ma'am."
"*How about five dollars? After all, I had to crawl*
Into a dark corner of that filthy butcher shop . . ."

III

When I get the parakeet home to the store,
I watch him struggle back to his cage-knowledge;
I think of the old maid handing him over,
Her tough hands tight on the five dollar bill,
Varicosed veins bulging in a world of age
Where she lives past her time in a rooming house
On social security that makes her scream at inflation.

IV

Weeks later . . . That parakeet refuses to be sold . . .
When I look at him secure, he stares back insecurity,
Everything small is watching everything large . . .
I feel my big head guarding things pea-shaped
And I wonder—Would the world level off flat
If you didn't have stupid guardians of size?
My parakeet just looks at me, watching me tall . . .
Some day I'll sell him, call her on the phone,
Tell her the parakeet has slipped away again,
And I'm not sorry to see that smallness go . . .

What's Wrong?

(A Running Conversation Between Two High School Girls on
the Way to the Bus)

"So what's wrong with Frankie
recommending books to read?"
    "Not five books a day!
    Five books in a row that guy
    told me I should try to read!"
"What's the matter with that?
What's wrong with reading five books?"
    "Look up with your silly eyes!
    Five books is like five clouds
    Sailing over your head . . .
    How do you know which cloud
    hits you or helps you with rain?"
"Why not learn to read clouds then?
Sail in the sky like a weatherman,
Sail high and free with those clouds!"
    "Don't bug me with your flying clouds.
    Things sail above you all the time.
    I want something up tight, near . . ."
"You want a man, that's what you want,
You want a man up tight and near . . ."
    "So what's wrong with a man
    instead of reading five books?
    You don't have to read a man . . ."

The Exterminator

I invade cheap apartment houses, 1920 dingy style,
Owned by absentee landlords who enjoy rents.
Early in the morning, scuffing faded, red carpets
That glitter with worn-out dreams of former wealth,
I saunter down dark corridors of dirty brown paint
And start pushing doorbells with prohibition slits
Where suspicion can stare out at fear when I ring
And call in my loud voice, "It's the Exterminator!"
I wait for the long pause, letting the words sink deep
Until they recognize it's only The Cockroach Man.
I catch them in all crazy, waiting positions,
Lovers in bed, housewives with their frizzled
Morning hair and pale, white lips before the paint of recognition;
Old people with their teeth out planning toothy smiles;
Shouting kids with toy guns and planes already at war.
I spray their garbage cans, run my hose up through
Broken plaster to liberate their walls with my poison.
These people don't like my early visits, but they need me
To stink up their places . . . Sometimes I get a cup of coffee
From a widow who keeps her pot steaming for gossip.
She talks about the rhythm of her life which has no beat . . .
I'd like to tell her some about the way of cockroaches,
Their crawling lives in walls around her, the way
They love to multiply, the way they die in my strong perfume . . .
But all I do is smell her cheap scent, listen to her chatter,
Sitting there in my clean, white uniform
Lettered with my name, *The Exterminator* . . .

In Today's Mirror: Dag Hammarskjold

"Two traits observed in today's mirror:
Ambitious—not in itself, perhaps, a fault.
but how short the step to pride or self-pity.
joyless—and a killer of joy."
        Dag Hammarskjold, *Markings*

My flesh no longer lures with expectation . . .
Joyless, am I really joy's killer? . . .
My youth was solitude, my family's country life,
A boy who found in loneliness the art of observation.
I loved to watch the poised ridiculous
Flare from prance of beasts and wildflower burst,
Wild energies to assert a gay, contrary color
Or a silly stance . . . My peering, lonely inquiries,
Sullenness, sudden laughter, fancied injuries,
Wrinkled in ambition's mask . . . Guilty, I grew
A guiltless face, a mask of casual, public confidence,
Wore a dark suit of service confining classical desires,
Grecian love of naked flesh, lived a careful calendar of costumes . . .
I learned how power's fused intensities stifle laughter,
How force intrudes when crisis finds no time for contemplation,
How dream-chained to their sexual myth of change
Statesmen stare from history's proud ruins as joy's killers . . .
In faded, legal documents, time's false monuments,
Joy lies buried, pleasure hides from social tasks,
Martyrs cannot laugh who have lost their satyr's flesh,
Their prancing feet . . . *Ambitious!* I strain for rhythm in the air . . .
I hear only a cold, even tread, a military march
That falls away in space . . . *Wish for joy's eccentricities!* . . .
I feel only the pressure of ambition's routine,
The day's patrolling duties that confine my hours . . .
In today's mirror I stare at my joyless face . . .
Slowly, I recognize joy's killer . . .

In 1970 in Madrid President Nixon Presents General Franco with a Red, White, and Blue Golf Bag, Clubs, and Twelve Autographed Golf Balls.

With this bag, General, it'll be like
Driving an American flag. Colors to make you blink,
Everything will glow so clear, so bright,
Down the fairway you'll go, straight down the middle,
Staying free from the rough to left and right . . .
When you bend over that ball, you'll find
A perfect lie. My name'll spring up
Shining whitely, an American president's name . . .
Maybe you dance a little Flamenco on it with your heel,
Maybe you cut it with your sword—that's all right too.
Your power's an old Spanish thing I learned about
As a boy in Southern California, where your Spanish Fathers
Converted all of us Indians with tobacco, cross, and guns.
It's great to see you still playing, a gamester at 77.
Golf is good for that old walk of authority,
Slice, hook, cut, blast out of the sandtrap,
Any trouble we drive into it's only a game
To conquer waterholes, a little smaller
Than the Mediterranean, right, but the same gleaming water
Over which our jets whiten your clear Spanish sky . . .
Here's to you, General, to our long international friendship.
I toast you striding sturdily on green grass,
Your Red, White, and Blue bag blazing before you,
A General of Games sparkling with pleasure's power.

Hog's Elegy to the Butchers

To Michael Anania

1

Here I come, Hog, the guitarist, to Chicago,
"Hog-Butcher to the world" they tell me it's called,
But that ain't where I got my big name.
Hog, 'cause when I lean over my guitar
My bulk clamps on the strings, man,
A savage weight, it's a hog playing,
Strumming, only my left hand finds
Princess fingers to free those chords
While my right hand drums hog-weight
Into the wood. Country boy to the big city,
You say, but it's country music they want to hear
As the big city eats high on hogs like me,
And that's why I'm coming to play
Them out of their drinks and their chatter . . .

2

My hotel says it's the biggest in the world
And I believe it, but the rooms are so small
They got gold prices on the wall measured in inches.
With my guitar I feel like I'm living
In sin we're so tight together in the bed.
No matter, the convention folks got to pay,
So I phone room service any time I want
To feed my guitar the corn-whiskey it likes.
People are running around the corridors
With badges from music stores all over the country.
This convention I'm playing is Holiday Time.
Now I know a convention is a money test—
Talk to any drunken stranger and find out
What simple music fits the climate of money.
Don't get too moody-deep, or the notes sink in cold air,

So I'll play 'em the old, driving country tunes
They like to think was played around the stove.
I'll go back home with my string tie sailing in the breeze.

3

Late afternoon with another rough guitar player
We come out of the hotel on our way to a drink.
Across the street in Grant Park sudden shots crack out
Like the usual school kid blast of firecrackers.
Half the city police, dressed and undressed,
Roar off the street onto park grass hell-bent
Through the trees for some red-hot target,
An ant pattern of furious energy cris-crossing
In a demon maze you never see except in dream.
Every boring day things happen under your nose
But you never know them. They whistle past your skin
Like a vulture cutting some invisible mouse
And you grin, wondering *what was that?*
How come I missed that cutting beak?
This time the mouse is some crazy guy from West Virginia
Out of World War II into mental hospitals,
In-patient, Out-patient is names they give him
When his mind starts shooting out rays of attack.
Why he comes to Chicago from his country cave
Is a guess of guns that he hides in his coat . . .
One police official says he came to kill the President
Who's scheduled to speak here tomorrow morning . . .
Another police official says there's no evidence
And maybe he was just going to kill himself . . .
Assassination or suicide, it's the same thing . . .
An idiot hider of guns, he drops one;
It clatters, glitters on the crowded sidewalk
And police chase him into the park. Radios close in;
They gun him down with a fierce, eager volley of shots—
So many shots no one knows who kills.
That's the way to keep your conscience strict—
Be a violent warrior for peace and justice.

69

You don't play with Chicago police, they believe
In that old frontier vision of dream-weapons.
In the crazy pockets of the guy they shoot
They find three pennies, a Bible, a pack of chewing gum . . .

4

That night I sing my Hog-elegy to any
Crazy thunder-power shining in the spotlights.
I hear myself sing wordlessly while ghost-music plays
Clamping on that wood I can't let go . . .
The ladies sit polite in their badges
And perfume from some strange world of manners
That's like a dam holding back crazy water . . .
They stop their gabbing suddenly to listen
To Hog-Power play this city out of my blood
'Cause my blood rejoices in that wild echo of guns . . .
Listen . . . It's better when I want to kill
If I kill with music . . . *You hear a man die* . . .
My guitar smokes with wild sounds, the strings
Turn green with fire, my fingers ache from slashing gut
And pounding wood, and they love me for that . . .
They clap, yell, crazy-happy for an encore from Hog . . .
All right, I'll play again . . . I'm gonna bust your ears . . .
You hear that rhythm driving loose? . . . *Who's playing?* . . .
A man with a Bible, three cents, a pack of gum . . .

Mr. and Mrs. Herman Melville, at Home, Isolated in Their Rooms

"Herman has taken to writing poetry.
You need not tell anyone,
For you know how such things get around,"
His wife writes to a friend . . .
She is sitting in her bedroom
Across from his study, worried about him.
He has taken to closing his door,
Shutting himself up, writing obscure poems,
A great manhole of isolation
With a peculiar, concealed look
That marks the losers of fantasy.
Some scholars laugh at her cautious words,
Some guess frustrations of sex, religion,
A somber, puritanical heritage, decorous duty
Masking, controlling the crawling visions . . .
Perhaps she also feels poetry is evil,
Dangerous, a possibility . . . Does she fear him
Closing the door, tense in his study,
Writing his labored, difficult poems? . . .
They are still there, sitting in history,
Wife and husband together, apart,
Disciplined boarders pursuing separate lives
In visionary, secluded rooms,
Worrying that poetry is
The shining grave of eternal language
That we write only to preserve
A myth of words opposed
To the acts of love.

Huck Finn at Ninety, Dying in a Chicago Boarding House Room

To give up everything . . .
Float away under the sun . . . .
The bliss of a bastard
Cut off from everyone . . .

To feel the Moms and Aunts
Pop their corsets like balloons
And the breasts of love
Soar out in white moons . . .

I sink back, a whiskey case,
Fondling the button I found—
"Make Love—Not War"—
In the park on the ground . . .

I've got the button, button . . .
Let me sleep in the gleam
Of that old raft floating down river
Through the frontier dream . . .

A Poet's Changing Inventory
for Walt Whitman: 1970

> *"Stock-taking, inventory, is the first effort of the
> mind to make itself at home . . . We see it in the
> Homeric catalogue and poetic inventory of Whit-
> man. But how does one do it where the home will
> not stay put? Where the stock of items on the shelves
> changes every day?"*
>
> Wright Morris, THE TERRITORY AHEAD

First-names, Walt, me to you, the American game
    of familiarity,
Camerado, Walt, Hart, and Jim converse
    as friends,
concealing force of last names,
false familiarity as a disease of yearning,
a mask for the companionship of isolation.

Once Paumanok, what is it about your names, your
    thing, Walt?
we know Long Island and its commuter-
    luxuries,
Paumanok has a wistful Indian tone
    of memory . . .
We killed most of them good, Walt,
    the Redskins,
why should a commuter long for a Redskin?

Ya-honk, the invitation of your wild gander leading
    his flock
through the night back into the frontier
    dream . . .
Ya-honk yourself, Walt. The Blacks call us
honkies now, metal aerials fly over Manhattan.

Pent-up, aching rivers, when you wandered
    the Mississippi,
  and reached New Orleans, did you feel the
    desire too
      to screw a slave, the guilty possession
      of bought flesh
  that haunts this country's sexual frustration,
  "from the warp and woof," your
    curious yearning,
  and yet you never really could sing
    "the body electric."
  "A woman's body at auction . . . she is
    the teeming
  mother of mothers . . ." What mothers, Walt?
  Is there a terrible purchase of mothers?

A woman waits for me . . . "They know how to
    swim, row, ride, wrestle,
  shoot, run, strike, retreat, advance, resist,
    defend themselves . . ."
  You talked yourself out of it, Walt,
    no one could
  keep it up with a woman of those qualities,
  did you want an Amazon, an aggression
    of force?

Me imperturbe, standing at ease in nature . . .
    aplomb in the midst
  of irrational things, anti-missile, anti-matter,
    anti-poetry,
  curse of the anti-spirit wrestling with the
    opposites,
  seeking the barbaric yawp over the roofs
    of the world.

The long line you gave us spreads out in a
    curious procession
  of persons and objects; eagle and cavalry,

low-hanging moons, solitary guests from
    Alabama,
slaves and masters, haunted homosexuals,
    isolated singers,
demons and birds, mechanics, journalists,
the noiseless, patient spider, the pure contralto
singing in the organ loft, the carpenter
    dressing his plank,
The driver with his interrogating thumb,
    "I give you
my love more precise than money,"
    wonderful cities
and free nations we shall fetch as we go on
    the open road
over the horizon to the end, the end of
    the frontier,
where you enter your Museum of History that
    I blow up
and the Good Grey Poet escapes from
    his camouflage
in the en-masse to reveal the cradle of liberty
    endlessly rocking.

"I hail with joy the oceanic, variegated, intense,
practical energy, the demand for facts, even the
business materialism of the current age, our States.
But woe to the age or land in which these things,
movements, stopping at themselves, do not tend
to ideas. As fuel to flame, as flame to the heavens,
so must wealth, science, materialism—even this
democracy of which we make so much—unswerv-
ingly feed the highest mind, the soul."

O Captain! My Captain! our fearful trip is done,
    but it's never done.
We scuttle backwards, crab-fashion, feeding
    our dream.

The footnote in the anthology says you meant
    Lincoln,
but I don't remember that Lincoln was ever
    a Captain.
Lashed by those confining oceans, Atlantic
    and Pacific,
We still ride secret ships of state into space.
Look up, Walt, we're about to escape to
    the moon!
My god, is all our land really a death-ship
where the hidden glory is to assassinate
    captains?
How come you wrote such a confidential
    cliché of a poem?
I'm afraid of your ship, Walt, your mysterious
    Captain . . .

Allons! Whoever you are come travel with me,
    traveling with me
you find *what never tires* . . . What never tires
    is a mystery Walt,
though, tired, we're still following the
    Democratic mystery,
perpetual journey, pursuit of happiness, joy
of wandering metal homes that never wait in
    time or space,
sense of motion that can only move,
    never return
except in the nostalgia of memory, the illusion
    of dream,
the Sleepers wandering in their night visions,
    probing
the darkness of dream worlds where all
    separations are immediate.

One of the roughs, a kosmos . . . eating, drinking,
    breeding . . .

I am one of your illegitimate word-children,
    Walt,
a bastard-poet lost in my kosmos, a rough,
although now the military scientists spell
    kosmos differently
and perform in it differently too . . .
I am wary of anonymous, technological
    astronauts . . .
Imagine Walt Whitman floating weightless
    in space!
That's my dream, Walt, old father of bastards,
we land on the moon and down the
    ladder comes
"disorderly fleshly and sensual," the man
    from earth
to present to the waste land of the moon
    the Song of Myself.

The Glorious Devil at the Dovecot:
Edgar Allan Poe and Sarah Helen Whitman

"I see by the *Home Journal* that your beautiful invocation has
reached the 'Raven' in his eyrie (at Fordham) and I suppose, ere
this, he has swooped upon your little dovecot in Providence. May
Providence protect you if he has! for his croak is the most eloquent
imaginable. He is in truth 'A glorious Devil, with large heart and
brain.'"

Mrs. Osgood to Mrs. Whitman

To Barton St. Armand

1—Sarah Whitman Conducting A Seance
In the dark, motionless,
A veil over my eyes
to enter the second darkness,
heavy velvet draperies
shielding forgotten flesh,
rich embroidered jacket
holding my age proud in time,
I wait for him to strike.
If he is a Glorious Devil, he will come.
The table trembles with soft sounds;
I listen for the lilt, snap of his voice,
after I wrote to tease him:
"A low bewildering melody
is murmuring in my ear . . ."
Bewildering shields the poison,
his shadow-mind's danger,
the *Doubt* which Lowell said
hides the secret of all horror,
the jealous play of loss that struck
with whispers of his infidelity,
a bitch-stranger courted in a nearby city
while he whispered to me of roses . . .
The table begins to move, the air of spirits listens . . .

Through the wood-cracks, the poisonous Doubt
flows out, escapes from our twined spirits.
Drink, drugs, his guillotine prose, knife-like tales,
fade into his poetry of praise.
We walk in the summer graveyard,
the Devil assumes his Glory,
and love breaks the earth to crystallize
the first dream of Helen of the Thousand Dreams . . .

2—*Poe: The Song in the Darkness*

In a timeless ear,
Love sings to the woman lost;
Doubt—Doubt is the spectre, Fear,
Master of the killing eye.
Let love break free from wagging tongues
That death looks down and cannot die . . .
The gossip and the spite rise up to haunt us.
Rumors, not earth-bound spirits move your table.
My croak is termed so eloquent; I am a Raven
sentenced to the mockery of *Nevermore.*
The President of Yale explains the refusal
of The Hall of Fame to admit me among its immortals:
"Poe wrote like a drunkard and a man
who is not accustomed to pay his debts."
Two lies. I wrote from my divided spirit
and from deep knowledge that debts are
never paid in money, only in a loss of love.
All that remains of me is false, pictures, words.
In a daguerrotype I'm shown untrimmed
with pasty skin, a mass of flaring hair,
satanic, proud mustache, a drooping eyelid
as though I squint at dream before reality,
one hand in my coat-front like a mocking actor,
an actor like my parents on their last debauch with time.
You listen . . . Do you hear? . . . *It's I singing my song,*
this drunkard attempting a search for love.
Do you think I prefer liquor, drugs, to flesh?
I'll knock your table out of your classical hand,

Helen, I'll sing you my glorious Devil's song:
Soft from the moving table
a dream is flowing
into nightmare, into love . . .
See, touch, its glowing . . .

3—Mrs. Whitman Clipping, Pasting In Her Scrapbook

Wear wild robes, ornaments against desolation,
shock the smart town with eccentricity,
behave with arrogance against time
because this life is too commonplace,
this Providence hides a difficult Providence . . .
What's left here? This picture of him drunk,
his vest unbuttoned, cravat whirling in mockery,
hair curling up short on his neck
where I asked him to cut a lock for me.
I keep this lock in my desk. It's a circle now.
It coils around and around to make its own planet.
Scraps, scraps . . . Obsessive flowers from tombs
To remind me of our summer cemetery walks,
a pansy that I picked from the grave of Keats,
a flower from the ruined Areopagus in Athens,
a daisy from a newly found ancestor's tomb—
Marguerite Le Poer—Power, my maiden name akin to her,
Power . . . Poer . . . Poe . . . I spend my failing time
searching lost names from graves in scrapbooks,
anagrams, puzzles, linking me forever with Poe—

S	A	R	A	H		H	E	L	E	N		P	O	E	R
3	6	5	1	2		8	4	9	10	11		7	12	14	13

1	2		3	4	5	6	7	8		9	10	11	12	13	14
A	H		S	E	R	A	P	H		L	E	N	O	R	E

4—Poe Walking Past The Deserted House Where Mrs. Whitman Died

Wild winter now,
bones of trees
break frozen flesh of snow.

Lost that sultry summer
in a forgotten year
when we met, loved
as roses reddened night
under the visionary stars.
A stranger is playing music
in your last, rented house
where you summon my spirit.
The dark blinds are down.
The house is empty . . .
Harpsichord fantasies
pursue ephemeral melodies,
voices from the eternal past
pluck frantically
for immortal sounds
while the music
pursues the wind.

5—*Mrs. Whitman With The Spirits*

He was a great magician, a God peer,
through whom the hisses of his soul flowed.
The spirits of Romance are separated by a unity
more real than that of martial complacency.
Baudelaire, Mallarmé . . . This French resurrection
of Poe which I helped create—the Raven spirit
spread as Manet drew his black-winged spectre . . .
What does this clipping say? "Baudelaire, like Poe,
died from artificial excitement . . ." The excitement of artifice . . .
Yet how create enduring artificial time,
time to cool that burning moment of failure
when harridan mother forced me to break our engagement,
hurled us forever apart, as I wept rejection
through my ether-scented handkerchief . . .
His suicidal nature plagued him after we parted . . .
With his alcohol, his pain-killing laudanum,
perhaps he was impotent . . . How could I save him with my flesh?
New England graves tremble with the guilt of touch;

we dress ourselves in fancy to flaunt our naked fears.
Husbands guard our safety, not our pleasure.
The risk was mine, as well as his, we faltered,
our nerve-ends of flesh failed to connect
despite a quick magic of tentative touch.
Yet the search for enduring spirit prevails . . .
In his firey moments of high inspiration
I listened to Poe when he no longer seemed mortal
but a spirit, a speaking, burning essence,
an alabaster statue melting into a white fire . . .
It is the fire that lives, burns the Raven into resurrection . . .

6—*Poe With The Actors*

The human brain leans to the Infinite
and fondles the phantom of the idea . . .
Seek me with the ghost company of actors,
I wear their masks, more comfortable than mine.
My lost parents dance their dressing room obsessions,
their sentimental, brief performances on stage
that masked a deeper, childless ritual they played—
and left to me the horror of weird tales . . .
I was born to wander from stage to stage,
to create phantoms in a haze of alcohol and drugs.
Somehow every actor always looks like me,
impoverished, dissolute, fake southern aristocrat
dragging, as I wrote in a story, my headless head,
my southern curse of nigger and poodle behind me;
scorning the genteel yet sucked into its world
to survive a little, play the gentleman's role,
leaving my vest unbuttoned purposefully for you
to capture your attention with my casual air . . .
My fate is to found a Theatre of Cruelty
that festers in the mind as well as on the stage.
Artaud, that fanatic Frenchman, who feels
The twitch of plague and magic, writes that he became
My character: "My life is that of Mr. Usher
and his sinister hovel. The soul of my nerves

is disease-ridden and I suffer from this . . ."
No wonder we are condemned to history, Sarah.
You love the actor for my act of love;
you fear the actor for my failed life.
One day in that trance of morning, where vision
blazes with its bright, blind eyes of wonder,
we will no longer read, play literary games,
we will watch my cruel words freeze into time.
As listeners we will step freshly out of books
into the world, the living, listening time
when defeated history stops its dream of action
and our new flesh begins at dawn for love.